GROW YOUR OWN

PET PLANTS

GROW YOUR OWN
PET PLANTS

Andrew Mikolajski
Photography by Peter Anderson

A cute guide
to choosing
and caring
for your
leafy friends

Smith
Street
Books

//CONTENTS

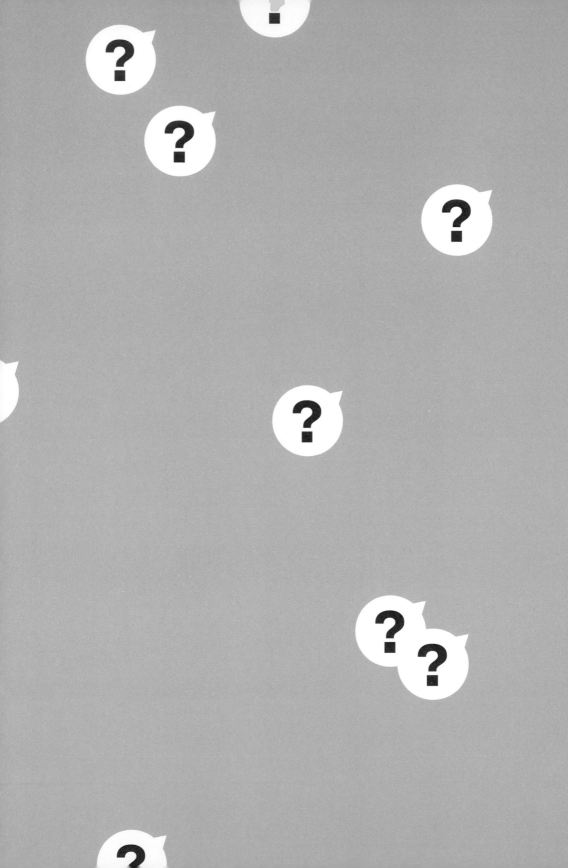

CHOOSING YOUR PETS

PLANT TYPES

So you've decided you'd like a pet but are dithering about which sort best meets your needs. Plants make great pets and, unlike the four-legged kinds, they will never annoy the neighbours or make a mess on the carpet, and you won't have to take them for walks — though some do like to go outside sometimes.

They will be there to greet you every time you come back home, sitting quietly exactly where you left them. Treated properly, plants will beautify your home or work space and reduce your stress levels.

perennial

PERENNIALS

Some plants are very leafy and look just like many of the ones you see in gardens — except most don't die back in winter, but stay looking good all year. They usually like it cool and shady, and those with very soft or textured leaves love being stroked.

tree/shrub

TREES & SHRUBS

Plants that have woody stems are sometimes big trees (or shrubs) in their natural habitat. However, they are usually much more restrained in captivity but can still be imposing. Obligingly obedient, these plants are generally tough and tolerant.

climbing/
trailing

CLIMBERS & TRAILING PLANTS

These elegant creatures either scramble skywards or — in the absence of a support — dangle their stems from up on high. They can be rather vigorous and often need some training (though you don't have to sign up to pet obedience classes).

FLOWERING PLANTS

These plants can be high maintenance. They usually need proper feeding and plenty of daylight if the flowers are to open fully — but too much direct light and they will scorch, especially if it's hot as well. Some flowering plants are ideal for temporary decoration and you can discreetly euthanise them once the flowers have faded.

Orchids

In the wild, many of these live in trees, clinging onto branches like monkeys. Moth orchids (Phalaenopsis) are very placid and easy to grow, but once you get hooked on them, you might be tempted by some of their more demanding relatives. Most of them like it cosy and warm.

orchid

FERNS

These are natural woodlanders, revelling in cool, damp situations. They like a nice shady spot at home and fortunately you don't have to turn the living room into a rainforest to keep them happy.

fern

CACTI & SUCCULENTS

These are like mini sculptures and just sit there, waiting to be admired. They like it hot and dry but need the right amount of water at the right time to keep them plump and healthy. They really don't like damp or humid air, but, unlike many other plants, they can often put up with draughts. Some are rather prickly characters, so should be handled with care.

cactus

BROMELIADS

A bit like the orchids, in the wild these spend their lives in trees or clinging to rocks. They often have thick leaves and are inclined to be spiky. This group includes the weirdly compelling air plants — plants that get all their sustenance from moisture in the air that they absorb through their leaves. They are your ultimate low-maintenance companion.

succulent

bromeliad

CHOOSING YOUR PETS

WHAT TYPE SUITS YOU?

Finding the right plants is a bit like finding the right boyfriend or girlfriend. You want one that will fit in with your lifestyle.

Jet-setting executive/corporate type

If you're out at work all day or spending long periods away from home, look for plants that don't mind drying out and will put up with some neglect. Cacti, succulents and air plants are often a good choice for commuters and anyone else whose home is largely a crash pad.

Homeworker

For people at home all day, why not try a pet that benefits from regular attention, such as an orchid? Any excuse to get up from the desk.

Stay-at-home-parent (SAHP)

Tough plants with thick leaves are ideal choices — they won't take up all your time and are largely child resistant. Cacti and other plants with prickles and spiky leaves are best avoided unless placed well out of reach of little fingers.

Boho, arty type/homemaker

If colour is your thing, flowering plants can match or complement your décor. Use them as you would cut flowers, moving them around as the fancy takes you.

Eco-warrior/environmentalist

If you love all things green and would like your living space to resemble some tropical jungle, go for some larger leafy plants and ferns.

Your living spaces

▶▶ A lot of plants like the same comfortable environment as you. Most enjoy an evenly lit spot, but not in direct sun, and a warm temperature, but not near a fire or radiator that can scorch their leaves.

▶▶ Many cannot abide low temperatures, especially when there are steep fluctuations between warm and cold, such as in a kitchen or bathroom.

▶▶ The majority don't like draughts, but there are some that relish fresh air.

▶▶ Make sure they don't catch a chill at night in winter. If they're near a window, either draw the curtains or move them away from the glass.

Minimalist/control freak

For that clean, pared-down look, why not try some of the cacti or bromeliads that look sculptural and don't grow very fast or have that annoying habit of shedding dead leaves everywhere? They make good arty shadows, too, if you light them properly.

Laid-back/easy-going drifter

If you like to take life as it comes, plants that trail casually from the bookshelves or tolerant trees and shrubs that can be allowed to gather dust in a corner might well suit you.

WHICH PET SHOULD YOU GET?

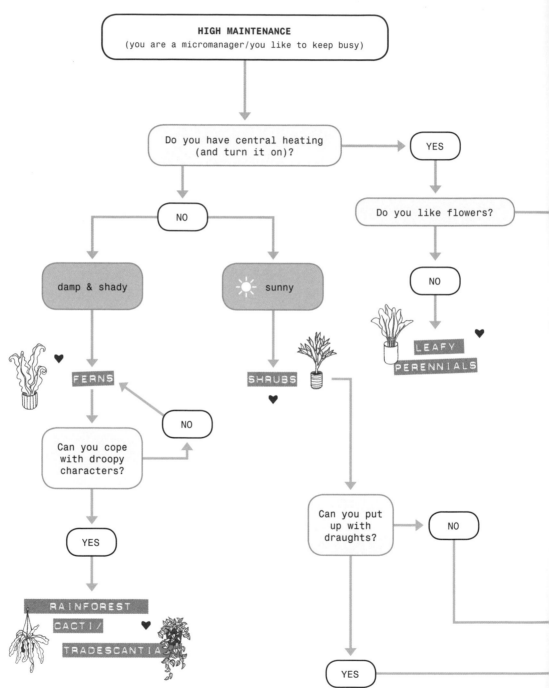

HIGH MAINTENANCE
(you are a micromanager/you like to keep busy)

Do you have central heating (and turn it on)?

YES

NO

Do you like flowers?

damp & shady

☀ sunny

NO

LEAFY PERENNIALS ♥

FERNS ♥

SHRUBS ♥

NO

Can you cope with droopy characters?

Can you put up with draughts?

NO

YES

YES

RAINFOREST CACTI / TRADESCANTIA ♥

CHOOSING YOUR PETS

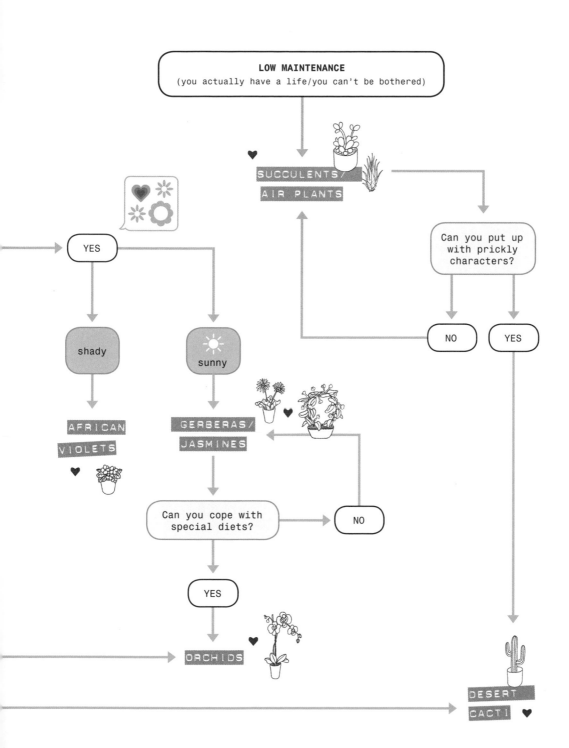

CHOOSING YOUR PETS

GETTING YOUR PETS HOME

Once you've decided what you want, you can head off in search of your new pet. Take some sturdy shopping bags or boxes with you, so they have a comfortable journey home.

Buying your pets

You can buy plants in garden centres, florists and supermarkets. Healthy ones will be clamouring for your attention. They should have bright green leaves and be largely symmetrical (apart from any flower stems they may be waving at you). Cacti, succulents and bromeliads should have firm leaves and stems with no wrinkling.

The compost surface should be clean, with no signs of fungal growth on it. If it's practical, check the plant's bottom — if there are roots poking through the holes in the underside of the container, the plant is 'pot-bound' and may struggle to grow once you've got it home.

Sometimes you see plants with 'reduced' stickers on them. Often bedraggled, with dead leaves and flowers, they look at you appealingly, begging you to pick them up and give them a home. If you are a new owner, you should really harden your heart as most of these won't survive for long. But if you have some experience with plants and are prepared to put in the effort, you can repot them and coax them back to health.

Are we there yet?

Plants don't mind being in the car (or other forms of transport), but they do need to stay cool. They're not afraid of the dark, so can go in the boot, standing upright rather than lying down. Wedge them in securely, so they don't fall over. Larger plants can stand in one of the footwells and you can keep your eye on them in the rear-view mirror. If plants do fall over and they're dry, they'll be sick, throwing up some or all of their compost over the floor.

It's best if leaves don't touch the windows, as they might scorch, but they also won't like the chilly draught blowing through an open window. If you have a long journey ahead of you and need to make a break, park in the shade and leave a window slightly open to stop them overheating. Remember that pets can die in hot cars.

Once you've got them home, you can get them used to their new living conditions. Give them a good drink of water and stand them in the kitchen sink or shower tray to drain for an hour or so while you decide where they'll be happiest in their new living quarters.

CHOOSING YOUR PETS

TIPS FOR SUCCESS //

▶▶ Choose healthy, symmetrical plants with plump green leaves.

▶▶ Avoid plants with roots growing out of the bottom of the pot or plants reduced for a quick sale.

▶▶ Keep the plants upright and cool on the way home; avoid strong sun and draughts.

▶▶ Once home, give them a good drink of water.

CARING FOR YOUR PETS

WATERING, FEEDING & GROOMING

Keep your plants happy and they'll show their appreciation with lots of healthy new growth. Neglect them and they might well show their disgust by dropping their leaves all over the floor.

Watering

Plants don't like being without water when they're actively growing — usually from spring to early autumn. Water the compost around the base of the plant, soaking it thoroughly. As a simple rule of thumb, water your pets every one or 2 weeks during this period, then reduce the frequency to once a month or so over winter, just to keep the compost moist. If your pet has fleshy or swollen stems or leaves, as cacti, succulents and some others do, you can allow them to dry out between winter waterings.

Most will be happy drinking tap water. Ideally, draw it 30 minutes before watering and let it come up to room temperature. If you live in a hard water area, splashes can dry to leave a calcium deposit on the leaves. You can boil the water first to get rid of this, then let it cool, like you do with a baby.

If you've got a lot of pets to deal with, to save time you can put them in the shower. They're not shy and will all quite happily stand together in the tray with the water on the cold setting. Alternatively, you can stand them all in a sink, basin or large tub full of water for 30 minutes or so until the compost is saturated. Allow them to drain completely.

During mild, wet weather, most of them like going outdoors for an hour or so — it firms up the leaves.

MISTING // Spraying rainforest plants with water makes them think they are in the tropics.

Feeding

Feeding plants keeps them healthy and strong. Feed during the growing period, usually spring–summer. Liquid fertilisers are easiest to use. Some have to be diluted and added to the water when watering. Others are ready to use, either watered into the compost or sprayed over the leaves.

Flowering plants, such as orchids, have special feeds. These contain a different balance of ingredients that encourages flower production.

Your pets don't need too much feeding, however, and less is better than more — overfeeding can make the stems droop.

Grooming

Your pets will love attention. To keep them looking their best at all times, remove any faded or withered leaves. Depending on the plant, you can either cut them off at the base with a pair of sharp scissors or snippers, use a small kitchen knife or pinch them out with your thumbnail.

You can buy special wipes or sprays for shining up smooth leaves — a sort of plant moisturiser. Most leaf shine products not only give leaves a healthy, polished look but also deliver a small amount of feed to the plant via the leaves.

Plants with hairy leaves sometimes attract dust and other detritus, so brush them gently with a paintbrush or old toothbrush to keep them clean.

CARING FOR YOUR PETS

BEDDING

When you buy your pets, they'll already be in containers filled with the right sort of compost. As they grow, you'll need to move them into bigger pots.

Houseplant compost

Standard houseplant compost contains a balance of ingredients and will suit many of your pets. You can also use a standard multipurpose compost, such as the compost used for outdoor plants in containers.

Cactus & succulent compost

Cactus compost is open and free-draining, with a high proportion of grit or fine gravel — important, because these plants absolutely hate having wet paws and will sulk if the compost is too damp.

Orchid compost

This barely looks like compost at all, essentially comprising bark chips and charcoal that keeps the mixture sweet smelling.

Bromeliad compost

Free-draining, this is based on composted bark, with added perlite (a lightweight, globular form of volcanic rock) and coir fibre.

CARING FOR YOUR PETS

TRIMS// While these aren't strictly necessary, a surface trim to the compost sets off the plant and can prevent water collecting around the base of stem — cacti and succulents in particular hate this. Moss will help keep ferns and other woodlanders nice and damp. Orchids are best without a trim, as the roots are adapted to exposure to the air.

Repotting a plant

When a plant fills its pot, it's time to move it into a larger one. It's a bit like changing a baby and can be messy, so it's best to do this over a sheet of thick plastic or on a kitchen surface that you can wipe down afterwards.

small stones

glass beads

1 Give your pet a thorough watering about 30 minutes before you start and let it drain. This makes the compost cling to the roots. Gently ease the plant out of its container.

pebbles

2 Put a few broken crocks, small stones or chunks of polystyrene at the base of the new container to cover the drainage holes. Top with a thin layer of fresh compost. Set the plant in the middle of the container.

gravel

sand

3 Fill around the perimeter of the plant with fresh compost, then firm it with your fingers — there should be a snug fit. A good drink of water will help settle your pet in its new home.

moss

CARING FOR YOUR PETS

SHOWING THEM OFF

If you want your pets to be happy, best find the right place for them in your home. Depending on what type they are, you can arrange them in groups or as singletons.

Placing your pets

· Cacti and other desert plants like sitting on a windowsill where they can see what's going on.

· Plants from tropical rainforests are happier in lower light levels, but if you want to place them where direct sun through glass will strike their leaves, screen the window with a sheer blind during hot weather in the summer.

CACHE POTS // Plants are nearly always sold in plastic pots that have holes in the base so water can drain through. Standing them in decorative pots ('cache pots') avoids embarrassing dribbles on the carpet when you water them. After watering, empty out any excess water at the base of the pot so your pet doesn't have to stand in a little pool of water.

· Trailers enjoy the vantage point of a high shelf from which they can peer down or can swing from the ceiling, suspended from hooks.

· Flowering plants like to preen themselves on a low table, inviting admiration from all angles.

 For well-balanced growth, keep turning your plants, as all of them have a tendency to crane their necks towards the window.

Grouping plants

Plants can be sociable creatures but tend to prefer their own kind. Most have a clear sense of their own personal space, so it's best if their leaves don't actually touch if you want to group them together. Too cramped and they can be susceptible to fungal diseases due to stagnant air collecting among the foliage.

Some can even sleep in the same bed. You can make a lovely arrangement of cacti or succulents together in a shallow bowl.

GLASS BOWLS //
Rainforest plants that like a damp environment can be displayed inside glass bowls. This not only raises the humidity around the plants but protects them from draughts.

1 Line the base of your container with polystyrene chips, then half-fill with cactus compost.

2 Take the plants out of their pots and arrange on the compost, then fill with more compost.

3 Top-dress with grit or a decorative trim.

SHOULD I BREED FROM THEM?

Unlike the four-legged kinds, your plant pets will never get embarrassingly randy in front of your guests. But many owners feel broody from time to time, and wonder if they can increase their stocks of plants. You don't need any special equipment, and any offspring will make excellent presents for your envious friends.

Taking stem cuttings

Plants with firm stems such as *Tradescantia* are easy to grow from cuttings. You can try this at any time of year, but cuttings taken in summer are usually the easiest to root.

1 Using a sharp knife, cut a short stem from the plant and trim off the lower leaves.

2 Place the cutting in water, so that the lower portion of the stem is immersed, while the leaves are above the surface.

Alternatively, pot the cuttings up around the edges of a 7 cm (3 in) pot filled with a mix of equal parts houseplant compost and grit, sand, perlite or vermiculite.

CARING FOR YOUR PETS

Removing offsets (aloes & others)

Some rosette-forming succulents spontaneously produce babies ('offsets') from around the base all on their own. It's worth detaching these and growing them on their own, because the mother plant loses vigour in the process of producing the new ones.

1 Using a sharp knife, detach the offsets, cutting as near to the base of the mother plant as possible. Trim the base of each offset, then let them dry out in a warm place for 24 hours. (This firms up the base of each offset.)

2 Pot up the offsets individually in small pots filled with a mix of equal parts houseplant compost and grit, sand, perlite or vermiculite. Top the mix with a layer of grit to prevent the rosette from rotting.

AFTERCARE //

 Keep all cuttings in a light-filled spot, but out of direct sunlight.

 Water cuttings in pots frequently so that they never dry out.

 For cuttings in water, change the water every 3 or 4 days.

 CUTTINGS // should root within about 4–8 weeks. In water, you will see the new roots clearly. For cuttings in pots, give each plantlet a gentle tug after a few weeks — if you feel resistance, roots are starting to form. Once they are well rooted, pot up the new plants individually in the appropriate compost.

HELP! — WHAT'S WRONG WITH MY PET?

There are no vets for plants. However carefully you tend them, your pets can sometimes show signs of pests and diseases, but at least you'll never be faced with extortionate vets' fees.

Preventing problems

✚ When you're buying plants, look for healthy specimens without any dead or dying leaves.

✚ Keep your pets fed and watered so they keep growing strongly.

✚ Remove dead leaves and flowers promptly — they can harbour disease.

 Sometimes just standing the plants outdoors for an hour or so can solve a problem. Beneficial outdoor insects will feed on any pests.

Exposure to fresh air can also get rid of any fungal or bacterial problems.

DEALING WITH SAD //

Just like you, your pets can feel a bit low during the darker months — seasonal affective disorder (SAD). You can perk them up by putting them under a mini growing lamp for a couple of hours each day. This is also a good way to encourage flowering plants to produce buds.

Dealing with pests

If you find your pet is covered with tiny insects, try one of the following:

✚ Wash off the pests by spraying the plants with water or standing them in the shower.
✚ Use a bug killer spray, following the manufacturer's instructions.
✚ Insert a sticky trap that catches the pests into the plant pot.

Dealing with diseases

Black spots or furry patches on leaves are signs of fungal or bacterial infection. Isolate any diseased plant from other plants to prevent the disease from spreading. Cut off all diseased parts of the plant. You can then spray with a plant fungicide, following the manufacturer's instructions.

Scale & honeydew

Scale insects are difficult to treat as they are covered with a shell or waxy or fluffy coating and cling like limpets to the stems of plants and undersides of leaves. Their secretions ('honeydew') drip down onto lower leaves, attracting fungus (sooty mould).You can remove the scales by hand, either by scrubbing with an old toothbrush or by wiping them off with a damp cotton swab. If only a section of the plant is affected, you can simply cut off that part.

The honeydew also attracts ants, which collect it to feed their young. In doing so, they transfer scale insect eggs from one part of the plant to another. To control the spread of scale insect, put down some ant traps around the plant.

Euthanasia
If your pet is really poorly, it can sometimes be wisest to put it out of its misery and consign it to the bin. Then you can go out and buy a replacement.

CARING FOR YOUR PETS

WE
JUST
LIKE TO
HANG
AROUND

EPIPHYLLUM ANGULIGER // FISHBONE CACTUS, ZIGZAG CACTUS

Unlike most other cacti, this fellow likes to stay cool and damp, lazily extending its paws in greeting. Treat it right and it will show its appreciation by pushing out an occasional scented flower.

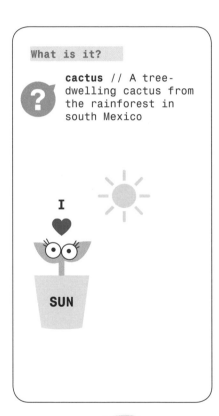

What is it?

cactus // A tree-dwelling cactus from the rainforest in south Mexico

I ♥ SUN

Take care of me...

Bright light but screened from direct sunlight through a window

Every 1–2 weeks from spring to autumn; keep just moist in winter

Apply a flowering houseplant or cactus fertiliser every 2 weeks in spring and summer

Remove faded flowers

For short periods during mild, damp weather in summer

No longer than 3 weeks from spring to autumn; up to 4 weeks in winter

COMPOST

Standard cactus compost

// Trim with moss to keep cool and moist

WE JUST LIKE TO HANG AROUND

SHRUBBY PERENNIAL

PELARGONIUM 'BALCONY LILAC' // IVY-LEAVED GERANIUM

With its lanky, jointed stems, this elegant creature is something of a thoroughbred and needs a certain amount of pampering to show off its best. Sulks without warm sunshine and proper feeding.

What is it?

shrubby perennial // A hybrid perennial bred from plants found in a variety of habitats in South Africa

I ♥ SUN

Take care of me...

 Full light near a window, but screened from hot sun in summer

 Every 1—2 weeks in spring and summer—autumn; every 3—4 weeks in winter

 Apply a flowering houseplant fertiliser every 2 weeks in spring and summmer

 Remove faded flowers

 Yes, during frost-free months

 No longer than 2 weeks from spring to early autumn; up to 4 weeks at other times

COMPOST

Standard household compost

// a trim of grit or sand is optional

WE JUST LIKE TO HANG AROUND

HEDERA HELIX // IVY

Quietly modest, this tolerant creature will put up with a certain amount of neglect and can even cope with quite dismal conditions. And it's obedient — you can teach it to climb up a support and cut it back if it seems to be getting out of control.

What is it?

climbing/trailing shrub // A trailing evergreen from lightly wooded areas of Europe; some forms have leaves marked with white or cream

I ♥ SHADE

Take care of me...

 Moderate to low light; types with patterned leaves need to be nearer a window but out of direct light

 Every 1—2 weeks in spring and summer; keep just moist at other times

 Apply a balanced houseplant fertiliser every 4 weeks in spring and summer

 Shorten any stems you think are too long

 Yes; they can usually stay outside all year

 No longer than 3 weeks in spring and summer; longer at other times

COMPOST

Standard household compost

// trim optional

WE JUST LIKE TO HANG AROUND

PERENNIAL

SCINDAPSUS PICTUS 'ARGYRAEUS'

// SATIN POTHOS, SILVER VINE

Treat it gently, and this quietly drooping character can be persuaded to lift its head up and climb. Otherwise, it likes to sit quietly on a shelf, gingerly dangling its spotty leaves but largely minding its own business.

What is it?

perennial // A trailing or climbing plant from tropical forests in Asia, northern Australia and the Pacific Islands

I ♥ SUN

Take care of me...

 Good light but screened from direct sunlight through a window

 Every 1–2 weeks in spring and summer, every 3–4 weeks in autumn and winter

 Every 4 weeks in spring and summer

 None necessary apart from removal of any dead leaves

 No

 No longer than 3 weeks in spring and summer

COMPOST

Standard houseplant compost

// trim optional

WE JUST LIKE TO HANG AROUND

FERN

PHLEBODIUM AUREUM // RABBIT'S FOOT FERN

This cool customer would love to swing from the chandeliers, or at least some conveniently placed hook, throwing out its bluish fronds from furry roots. Unlike most other ferns, it can put up with dry air — so long as it gets enough to drink.

What is it?

 fern // A rock- or tree-dwelling fern from the southern USA and parts of tropical South America

I ♥

SUN

Take care of me...

 Bright light but screened from strong sunlight through a window

 Every 2–3 weeks during spring and summer, every 6 weeks in autumn and winter

 Every 4 weeks in spring and summer

 Remove any fronds that turn brown

 During mild, still weather in the warmer months

 Up to 4 weeks, or longer in winter

COMPOST

 Equal parts standard houseplant compost and sand

// a moss trim will help keep the roots cool

WE JUST LIKE TO HANG AROUND

TRADESCANTIA ZEBRINA // SILVER INCH PLANT

A plant that likes to mooch languidly around, dangling its purplish, slightly hairy stems and purple-and-silver striped leaves — as though it can't be bothered to get out of bed and have a shave. Occasionally summons up the energy to push out a few small flowers.

What is it?

perennial // A trailing perennial from scrubby and wooded parts of southern Mexico

Take care of me...

☀ Bright light, which intensifies the leaf colour, but screened from hot sun

💧 Weekly in spring and summer; less at other times

🍽 Every 4 weeks in spring and summer

✂ Shorten overlong stems, if necessary

🚪 Yes, for prolonged periods in summer if sheltered from the hot midday sun

🧳 No longer than 2 weeks

Standard houseplant compost

// trim optional

WE JUST LIKE TO HANG AROUND

WE
MUST BE
THE
GLAMOURPUSSES
CENTRE
OF
ATTENTION

PERENNIAL

SAINTPAULIA // AFRICAN VIOLET

A real sweetheart of a pet, with jewel-like flowers clustered on sturdy stems above velvety, strokable leaves. Desirable, but inclined to be high maintenance: fussy feeders, they need repotting every year.

What is it?

perennial // A plant bred from evergreen perennials found in damp areas of tropical East Africa with white, pink, red, blue or purple flowers

I ♥ FOOD

Take care of me...

 Good light but screened from direct sunlight through a window; full light in winter (use a growing lamp)

 Every 1—2 weeks in summer; keep just moist at other times; water around the base of the plant, not above

 Apply a flowering houseplant fertiliser every 2 weeks during summer

 Remove faded flowers and leaves promptly

 No

 For short periods only during summer; longer at other times

COMPOST

Standard houseplant compost

// trim optional

WE MUST BE THE CENTRE OF ATTENTION: GLAMOURPUSSES

PERENNIAL

ANTHURIUM ANDREANUM // FLAMINGO FLOWER

Here is the most brazen attention seeker, flaunting its reproductive parts in the most shameless way. Very good at parties, it likes being the centre of attention and is a great conversation starter.

What is it?

perennial // A tree-dwelling perennial with glossy, usually red flowers from wet mountain forests of Colombia and Ecuador

I ♥ SHADE

Take care of me...

 Moderate light but away from direct light through a window

 Every 1–2 weeks in spring and summer; keep just moist at other times

 Apply a balanced fertiliser every 2–3 weeks in spring and summer

 Remove faded flowers; apply leaf shine to leaves

 No

 No longer than 2 weeks in spring and summer; longer at other times

COMPOST

Standard houseplant compost with added sand

// trim with moss to keep the roots damp

WE MUST BE THE CENTRE OF ATTENTION: GLAMOURPUSSES

CALATHEA/GOEPPERTIA CROCATA 'TASSMANIA'
// ETERNAL FLAME

This glamorous creature looks ready for a night out and likes sitting in the middle of a room, so it can be admired from all angles. Terrified of getting any more wrinkles, it hates being too near the window or any other dry heat source and cannot abide draughts. Would probably prefer to sit in a sauna all day, given the chance.

What is it?

perennial // An evergreen perennial from tropical rainforest in the Americas

I ♥ STROK-ING

Take care of me...

 Bright light but away from direct sunlight through a window

 Every 1–2 weeks in spring and summer; mist daily; water more sparingly at other times

 Apply a balanced fertiliser every 4 weeks in spring and summer

 Remove any faded leaves

 No

 Up to 2 weeks in spring and summer; longer at other times

COMPOST

Standard household compost

// a bead trim can help keep the roots moist

WE MUST BE THE CENTRE OF ATTENTION: GLAMOURPUSSES

Suitable
for: ♥ ♥ ♥

High-maintenance
types with
an advanced
skincare regime

PERENNIAL

GERBERA JAMESONII // TRANSVAAL DAISY

Naturally sweet-natured, gerberas will light up any room, but tend to turn their faces towards the sun. In fact, they love going outside in warm weather. Best not get too attached to them, though — they're not very long-lived.

What is it?

perennial // A short-lived perennial with daisy-like red, yellow, pink or cream flowers from areas of grassland in South Africa and Swaziland

I ♥ SUN

Take care of me...

Bright light but screened from strong sunlight through a window

Weekly, whenever flowers (or buds) are present; every 3–4 weeks at other times

Apply a flowering houseplant fertiliser every 4 weeks in spring and summer (or when flowering at other times)

Cut back stems bearing faded flowers to the base

Yes, and it can stay out all night provided the temperature stays above freezing

Only up to 1 week when flowering; up to 2 weeks at other times

COMPOST

Standard houseplant or multi-purpose compost

// a trim of decorative beads can enhance its appeal

52

WE MUST BE THE CENTRE OF ATTENTION: GLAMOURPUSSES

Suitable
for:
Spontaneous types
likely to fall
in love with
these endearing
creatures at
first sight

CALLA/ZANTEDESCHIA // CALLA LILY

Unlike other houseplants, this one actually hibernates, shedding its spotty leaves at the end of summer, then having a good rest before emerging again in spring. Loves a drink while it's up and about.

What is it?

perennial // A perennial from lake margins and swamps in south and east Africa; flower colours include white, pink, red, orange, yellow and dark purple

I ♥ A GOOD REST

zzzzzzz

Take care of me...

Full light but screened from strong sunlight through a window

Weekly in spring and summer; stop watering when the leaves start to die back, then keep dry over winter

Apply a balanced fertiliser every 2 weeks in spring and summer

Gently pull away collapsed leaves in autumn

Yes, during frost-free months

Up to 2 weeks in spring and summer; can be left entirely alone in winter

COMPOST

Standard household compost

// trim optional

WE MUST BE THE CENTRE OF ATTENTION: GLAMOURPUSSES

ORCHID

CAMBRIA //

Tall and willowy, this lanky creature would lurk unnoticed were it not for its knockout scent, so don't hide it away. The flower stem needs tying to a cane to stop it keeling over.

What is it?

orchid // An epiphytic orchid bred from a range of different plants found in mountainous regions of the southern USA and Central and South America

Take care of me...

 Bright light but screened from direct sunlight through a window

 Every 1–2 weeks in spring and summer; sparingly at other times

 Apply an orchid fertiliser every 2–3 weeks in spring and summer (and at other times, if flowering)

 Remove faded flowers

 No

 No longer than 3 weeks in spring and summer (or when flowering)

COMPOST

Orchid compost

// no trim required

WE MUST BE THE CENTRE OF ATTENTION: GLAMOURPUSSES

ORCHID

DENDROBIUM //

Cool and sophisticated, these tricky creatures are real eye-catchers when their upright stems are covered in flowers. Trouble is, they like to be kept literally cool, and need frequent misting to stop them overheating. They also like cramped conditions in their pots.

What is it?

orchid // An orchid bred from tree-dwelling plants found in tropical rainforest in south and east Asia and Australia with white, pink and yellow flowers

I ♥ FOOD

Take care of me...

 Light shade in spring and summer; full light in autumn and winter

 Weekly from spring to autumn; mist regularly to keep plants cool; keep dry in winter

 Apply an orchid fertiliser every 2–3 weeks in spring and summer

 Remove faded flowers

 No

 No longer than 2 weeks when flowering; longer in winter

COMPOST

Standard orchid compost

// no trim required

WE MUST BE THE CENTRE OF ATTENTION: GLAMOURPUSSES

SUCCULENT

KALANCHOE BLOSSFELDIANA // FLAMING KATY

Looking a bit like a mini tree, this waxy-leaved, picture-book character will spark joy in your life when it's topped with clusters of white, yellow, pink, red or orange flowers. Very good with children.

What is it?

succulent // A succulent perennial from semi-desert areas of Madagascar

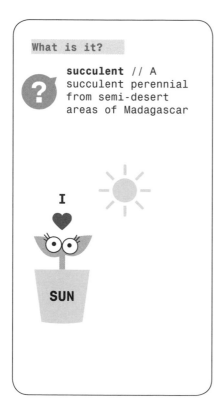

Take care of me...

 Good light but screened from strong sunlight through a window

 Every 2–3 weeks in spring and summer; at other times, keep just moist

 Apply a balanced fertiliser every 4–5 weeks in spring and summer

 Remove faded flowers

 No

 Up to 3 weeks in spring and summer; longer at other times

COMPOST

Standard houseplant compost with added grit (2:1)

// trim with grit or sand to keep the base of the stems dry

WE MUST BE THE CENTRE OF ATTENTION: GLAMOURPUSSES

GUZMANIA LINGULATA // SCARLET STAR

This vibrant fun-seeker gains attention by thrusting skywards a brilliant, glowing orange flower from inside a rosette of leathery, strappy leaves.

What is it?

 bromeliad // An epiphytic bromeliad that flowers in summer and found mainly in the Andean rainforest

I ♥
MIST

Take care of me...

 Good to moderate light, screened from direct sunlight through a window

 Water only occasionally, keeping the compost just moist; mist daily in spring and summer

 Mist with a balanced liquid fertiliser every 2 weeks in spring and summer

 Remove any dead leaves from the outside of the plant

 No

 No longer than 2 weeks in spring and summer; longer at other times

COMPOST

 Standard bromeliad compost/orchid compost

// a trim of beads, pebbles or stones will keep the base of the plant dry

WE MUST BE THE CENTRE OF ATTENTION: GLAMOURPUSSES

WHAT ABOUT US? WE ALSO NEED A BIT OF PAMPERING

FERN

ADIANTUM RADDIANUM 'FRAGRANS' // MAIDENHAIR FERN

Tossing its locks in the slightest breeze — it doesn't mind a draught — this elegant creature will sit demurely to the side of a room, even near a doorway. Brush it lightly with your hand whenever you pass by.

What is it?

fern // An evergreen fern with bright green fronds from damp, tropical areas of the Americas

Take care of me...

 Bright light but away from a window; tolerates lower light levels

 Every 1–2 weeks in spring and summer; more sparingly at other times (without letting the plant dry out)

 Apply a balanced fertiliser at half strength every 4 weeks in spring and summer

 Remove any brown fronds in spring

 No

 Up to 3 weeks in spring and summer; longer at other times

COMPOST

Equal parts houseplant compost and limestone gravel

// trim with moss to keep the roots damp

WHAT ABOUT US? WE ALSO NEED A BIT OF PAMPERING

PERENNIAL

CHLOROPHYTUM COMOSUM 'VITTATUM' // SPIDER PLANT

Easy to please, a spider plant can sit near a window or further away on shelving. You'll wonder how you ever lived without it. Happy plants fling out long stems bearing new plantlets at the tips.

What is it?

perennial // A perennial with strappy leaves from forest margins in tropical Africa

I ♥
FOOD

Take care of me...

 Bright light but screened from direct sunlight through a window; tolerates lower light levels

 Every 1–2 weeks in spring and summer; keep the compost just moist at other times

 Apply a balanced fertiliser every 4 weeks in spring and summer

 Pinch out any brown leaf tips

 During warm periods in summer only

 Up to 3 weeks in spring and summer; longer at other times

 COMPOST

Standard houseplant compost

// trim optional

WHAT ABOUT US? WE ALSO NEED A BIT OF PAMPERING

ASPLENIUM NIDUS // BIRD'S NEST FERN

This quiet, unobtrusive creature is a calming presence and loves just to sit in a glass bowl or terrarium where it can stay cool and damp, though it can also be grown in pots. In the wild, rainwater and organic detritus collect in the middle of the plant.

What is it?

 fern // A rosette-forming evergreen fern from tropical areas of the globe, where it grows on organic matter, sometimes among tree branches above ground level

I ♥ DAMP

Take care of me...

 Moderate to low light, away from bright sunlight

 Every 1–2 weeks in spring and summer; mist daily (pot-grown plants); water more sparingly in winter

 Apply a balanced fertiliser at half strength every 4 weeks in spring and summer

 Remove dead fronds

 No

 No longer than 2 weeks in spring and summer; longer at other times

COMPOST

 Standard houseplant compost with added sharp sand (2:1)

// trim with moss to keep the roots cool (pot-grown plants)

WHAT ABOUT US? WE ALSO NEED A BIT OF PAMPERING

PERENNIAL

CODIAEUM VARIEGATUM // CROTON

With its spotted leaves, this creature could almost pass as the spotted laurel you see in gardens but has a guilty secret — its sap is poisonous. Best not to provoke it by attacking it with the secateurs. Hates being in a draught.

What is it?

perennial // A shrubby perennial from open woodland and scrub in Malaysia and other parts of the Western Pacific region; some forms have striped or patterned leaves

I ❤ SUN

Take care of me...

 Full light but screened from direct sunlight through a window

 Every 1—2 weeks in spring and summer; mist regularly; in autumn and winter; water to keep compost just moist

 Apply a balanced fertiliser every 2—3 weeks in spring and summer

 Carefully remove any faded leaves

 No

 Up to 2 weeks in spring and summer; longer at other times

COMPOST

Standard houseplant compost

// trim with moss to help keep the roots moist

WHAT ABOUT US? WE ALSO NEED A BIT OF PAMPERING

PERENNIAL

DIEFFENBACHIA SEGUINE // DUMB CANE

This tolerant creature can put up with a range of conditions but needs handling with care — the sap that bleeds from damaged stems can be a skin irritant, so don't treat it too roughly. The lower leaves are shed periodically, leaving scars on the stem.

What is it?

 perennial // A firm-stemmed perennial with large paddle-shaped leaves, which are variously spotted, striped or streaked with cream or yellow

I ♥ MIST

Take care of me...

 Bright light but away from direct sunlight; full light in winter

 Every 1–2 weeks in spring and summer; mist daily in summer; water more sparingly at other times

 Apply a balanced fertiliser every 4 weeks in spring and summer

 None required

No

 Up to 3 weeks in spring and summer; longer at other times

COMPOST

 Standard houseplant compost with added sharp sand (3:1)

// trim optional

WHAT ABOUT US? WE ALSO NEED A BIT OF PAMPERING

Suitable
for: ♥ ♥ ♥

Considerate people
sensitive to the
needs of other
living things

PERENNIAL

DIONAEA MUSCIPULA // VENUS FLY TRAP

This snappy creature is bound to be a talking point. Impress your friends by getting it to do its party trick — eating live house flies. It loves paddling in the summer then dies off completely and takes a winter rest.

What is it?

perennial // A carnivorous, rosette-forming perennial with spine-bearing leaves from boggy areas of the Carolinas

Take care of me...

 Bright light but screened from direct sunlight through a window

 Keep permanently wet in spring/summer, or stand in a saucer of water; keep just moist at other times

 Unnecessary; plants trap their own food

 Remove 'traps' as they blacken and die back in autumn

 No

 Up to 3 weeks provided it can be kept damp

COMPOST

A mix of equal parts moss peat and lime-free sand

// a trim of moss can help raise humidity

WHAT ABOUT US? WE ALSO NEED A BIT OF PAMPERING

PERENNIAL

MARANTA LEUCONURA 'ERYTHROPHYLLA' // PRAYER PLANT

This sensitive creature shuns bright light and likes a shallow container, as its roots don't go very deep. The silky-textured, tabby leaves are lovely to stroke, but sensitive, turning crisp with too much sunlight or fluctuation in temperatures.

What is it?

 perennial // A leafy perennial from tropical rainforests of the Americas

Take care of me...

 Indirect light away from strong sunlight through a window

 Every 1–2 weeks in spring and summer; keep just moist at other times

 Apply a balanced fertiliser every 4 weeks in spring and summer

 Remove any dead leaves

 No

 No longer than 3 weeks in spring and summer; longer at other times

COMPOST

 Standard houseplant compost

// trim optional

WHAT ABOUT US? WE ALSO NEED A BIT OF PAMPERING

TREE/SHRUB

DRACAENA MARGINATA // MADAGASCAR DRAGON TREE

Looking like a mini palm tree, this scruffy creature is no trouble at all. It doesn't grow very fast, so won't keep taking up more space. You can even take it to the office with you — and leave it there.
It's reputedly good at clearing the air.

What is it?

tree/shrub // An evergreen shrub or tree with long, narrow, olive-green leaves from scrubby areas of Réunion

Take care of me...

 Full light but screened from direct sunlight through a window; tolerates lower light levels

 Every 1–2 weeks from spring to autumn (though tolerates less frequent watering); sparingly in winter

 Apply a balanced fertiliser every 4 weeks in spring and summer

 Pinch out any leaf tips that turn brown

 Yes, in summer

 Up to 4 weeks; can be allowed to dry out between waterings

COMPOST

Standard houseplant compost

// trim optional

WHAT ABOUT US? WE ALSO NEED A BIT OF PAMPERING

TREE/SHRUB

FICUS ELASTICA // RUBBER PLANT

'Tall, dark and handsome' sums up this über-smooth dude, which can strut its stuff in a corner, towering over smaller fry and shading them out with its big, leathery leaves. Fancies itself in a tuxedo or even a smoking jacket.

What is it?

tree/shrub // An evergreen tree from tropical forests of the eastern Himalayas and surrounding region

Take care of me...

 Tolerant of both strong sunlight and lower light levels

 Every 1–2 weeks in spring and summer, every 2–3 weeks in autumn and winter

 Apply a balanced fertiliser every 4 weeks in spring and summer

 Keep the leaves glossy with regular applications of leaf shine

 During warm periods in summer

 No longer than 3 weeks in spring and summer; up to 4 weeks at other times

COMPOST

Standard houseplant compost

// trim optional

WHAT ABOUT US? WE ALSO NEED A BIT OF PAMPERING

MUSA ACUMINATA // BANANA

Bringing an old-fashioned colonial style to any interior, a banana palm is quietly imposing but needs space, as it grows quite tall. Kept warm and happy, it might even present you with a bunch of bananas from time to time.

What is it?

perennial // A palm-like plant from light woodland in warm areas of Japan with huge, thin-textured, paddle-shaped leaves that tend to split as they age

I ♥ SUN

Take care of me...

 Full light but screened from direct sunlight through a window

 Every 1–2 weeks in summer; keep just moist at other times

 Apply a balanced fertiliser every 4 weeks in spring and summer

 Remove any leaves that turn brown

 Yes, in summer, but can be susceptible to wind damage

 Up to 2–3 weeks in spring and summer; longer at other times

COMPOST

Standard houseplant compost

// trim optional

WHAT ABOUT US? WE ALSO NEED A BIT OF PAMPERING

PERENNIAL

PEPEROMIA MARMORATA // SWEETHEART PEPEROMIA

This diminutive creature doesn't take up much space and will look after itself, once you have found the right spot for it — too much light and it will scorch, too little and it will lose colour and fade away.

What is it?

 perennial // A rosette-forming perennial with heart-shaped, grey-green leaves from tropical rainforest in Central and South America

Take care of me...

 Indirect light in spring and summer; bright light in autumn and winter

 Every 1—2 weeks in summer; mist daily in spring and summer; water less frequently at other times

 Apply a balanced fertiliser every 4 weeks in spring and summer

 Remove any faded leaves

 No

 Up to 2 weeks in summer; longer at other times

COMPOST

 Standard household compost

// a moss trim can help maintain humidity

WHAT ABOUT US? WE ALSO NEED A BIT OF PAMPERING

CHOOSE
CUTE

TREE/SHRUB

YUCCA ELEPHANTIPES // GIANT YUCCA, SPINELESS YUCCA

Into sword-fighting, this character is excellent at warding off intruders, poking them in the eye with its pointed, blade-like leaves if they get too close. Approach with caution.

What is it?

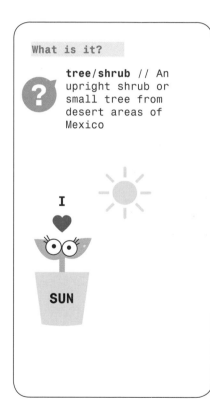

tree/shrub // An upright shrub or small tree from desert areas of Mexico

Take care of me...

 Full light

 Every 2—3 weeks in spring and summer; at other times, water only to prevent the compost from drying out

 Apply a balanced fertiliser every 4 weeks in spring and summer

 Apply leaf gloss to leaves

 Yes, in spring and summer

 Up to 4 weeks

COMPOST

Standard household compost

// trim with grit or small stones to keep the base of the trunk dry

WHAT ABOUT US? WE ALSO NEED A BIT OF PAMPERING

PERENNIAL

SANSEVIERIA TRIFASCIATA // MOTHER-IN-LAW'S TONGUE

Possibly unlike your partner's parents, this unfussy plant never interferes. It will happily sit in the same pot for several years without complaining, and you only need to rehouse it when it literally cannot grow any more.

What is it?

perennial // An evergreen perennial with thickened, upright, leathery leaves found among rocks in warm parts of Africa, India and Indonesia

Take care of me...

 Bright light but screened from direct sunlight through a window; can tolerate lower light levels

 Every 2 weeks in spring and summer; keep just moist at other times

 Apply a balanced fertiliser every 4 weeks in spring and summer

 None required

 For short periods in mild weather in summer

 No longer than 3 weeks in spring and summer; longer at other times

COMPOST

Standard houseplant compost with added grit (2:1)

// trim optional

WHAT ABOUT US? WE ALSO NEED A BIT OF PAMPERING

WE JUST SIT THERE...

ALOE ARISTATA 'COSMO'

A reptilian creature with sculptural, tough, pointed leaves that's happy to sit quietly on a low table or shelf, making few demands and not eating or drinking very much or complaining about draughts. Likes to spend time on its own, like Garbo.

What is it?

succulent // A rosette-forming succulent with thickened, pointed, spiny-edged leaves from desert regions of southern Africa

I ♥ SUN

Take care of me...

 Bright light but screened from direct sunlight through a window

 Every 1—2 weeks in spring and summer; less frequently in winter

 Apply a balanced fertiliser 2 or 3 times during spring and summer

 Remove dead leaves from around the base of the plant

 For a short time during warm, dry periods in summer

 No longer than 3 weeks in spring and summer; up to 4 weeks or more at other times

COMPOST

Standard cactus compost

// a trim of grit, stone chippings or beads will keep excess moisture off the base of the plant

WE JUST SIT THERE...

CACTUS

ASTROPHYTUM MYRIOSTIGMA // BISHOP'S CAP

A venerable creature that exudes a self-satisfied pomposity but is really no trouble to keep happy. Prone to flamboyance in summer, when it pushes out large yellow flowers.

What is it?

cactus // A slow-growing cactus, covered with whitish scales, from arid regions of the southern USA and Mexico

I ♥ SUN

Take care of me...

 Full light with some screening from strong sun through a window

 Every 1–3 weeks in spring and summer; keep dry at other times

 Apply a standard cactus compost every 4 or 5 weeks in spring and summer

 None required

 No

 Up to 3 or 4 weeks in spring and summer; longer at other times

COMPOST

Standard cactus compost with added grit (2:1)

// trim with grit or sand to keep the base dry

96

WE JUST SIT THERE...

SUCCULENT SHRUB

CRASSULA OVATA // MONEY PLANT

This easy-to-care-for plant needs very little attention and quietly gets on with the business of growing, like a pension. Given time, it becomes a mini tree. Easy to build up stock from, as cuttings root easily.

What is it?

succulent shrub // A tree-like, branching succulent with bright green, fleshy leaves from dry areas of South Africa and Mozambique

Take care of me...

 Full light but screened from strong sunlight through a window

 Every 2–3 weeks in spring and summer; at other times, water only to prevent the compost drying out

 Apply a cactus fertiliser every 4 weeks in spring and summer

 None required

 During mild, dry weather in summer

 Up to 4 weeks at any time

COMPOST

Standard cactus compost

// a trim of grit, sand or stone chippings will keep the base of the stems dry

WE JUST SIT THERE...

 SUCCULENT

ECHEVERIA SETOSA VAR. DEMINUTA
// MEXICAN FIRECRACKER

This little plant is like an indoor firework, sparking up clusters of bright red and yellow flowers throughout the summer.

What is it?

 succulent // A rosette-forming succulent with thick, greyish green leaves from desert and other dry regions of Mexico

Take care of me...

 Full light but screened from strong sunlight through a window

 Every 1–2 weeks in spring and summer; keep barely moist at other times

 Apply a cactus fertiliser every 4 weeks in spring and summer

 Remove faded flowers, cutting the stem to the base

 During warm, dry periods in summer

 Up to 3 weeks in spring and summer; up to 4 or 5 weeks in autumn and winter

COMPOST

 Standard cactus compost

// trim with grit or sand to keep the base of the plant dry

WE JUST SIT THERE...

SUCCULENT

EUPHORBIA TRIGONA // AFRICAN MILK TREE

Looking a bit like a cactus, but with leaves, this impressive succulent has an air of self-importance. But it has a deadly secret — there's a pair of little spines lurking beneath each leaf.

What is it?

succulent // A column-forming, tall-growing, bright green succulent that forms dense thickets in parts of central Africa

Take care of me...

 Bright light but screened from direct sunlight through a window

Every 1–2 weeks in spring and summer; allow to dry out between waterings at other times

Apply a cactus fertiliser every 4 weeks in spring and summer

None required

During warm, dry periods in summer

Up to 3 or 4 weeks in spring and summer; longer at other times

COMPOST

Standard houseplant compost with added grit (3:1)

// trim with gravel or chippings to keep the base of the stems dry

WE JUST SIT THERE...

GYMNOCALYCIUM MIHANOVICHII 'RED HEAD'
// MOON CACTUS, RUBY BALL CACTUS

This freak of nature hardly looks like a living plant at all — but it is, though it's created artificially. Also available in pink, yellow and orange.

What is it?

cactus // This mutant cactus comes from South America. Lacking chlorphyll (green pigment), it survives only by being grafted on top of a different cactus (usually Hylocereus)

Take care of me...

 Full light but screened from strong sunlight through a window

 Every 1–2 weeks in spring and summer; keep dry at other times

 Apply a cactus fertiliser every 4 or 5 weeks in spring and summer

 None required

 No

 Up to 3 weeks in spring and summer; longer at other times

COMPOST

 Standard cactus compost

// trim with grit or sand to keep the base of the plant dry

WE JUST SIT THERE…

CACTUS

MAMMILLARIA HAHNIANA // OLD LADY CACTUS

Not quite so hairy as the old man of the Andes cactus, the old lady cactus makes a good companion for him — and you won't be overrun with baby cactuses, as they are both past it.

What is it?

cactus // A spherical, spiny cactus, covered with short, white hairs, from semi-desert regions of central Mexico; flowers in spring and summer

Take care of me...

 Full light but screened from strong sunlight through a window

 Every 1–2 weeks from mid-spring to autumn; in winter, allow to dry out between waterings

 Apply a cactus fertiliser every 4 weeks from mid-spring to end of summer

 Gently brush the hairs to get rid of dust and other detritus

 During warm, dry periods only

 Up to 4 weeks in spring and summer, longer at other times

COMPOST

Standard cactus compost

// trim with grit, small stones or beads to keep the base of the plant dry

WE JUST SIT THERE…

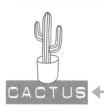

 CACTUS

OREOCEREUS TROLLII // OLD MAN OF THE ANDES

This venerable being will sit sagely on a windowsill, watching life go by. It's generally good-natured and tolerates having its hair gently brushed with an old toothbrush, but don't get too close or it might stab you with its prickles. It hates getting its hair wet, so don't water it from overhead or stand it in a shower.

What is it?

 cactus // A cactus forming short columns, from dry, mountainous regions of Bolivia and Argentina

I ♥ HAIR -DOS

Take care of me...

 Full light but screened from direct sunlight through a window

 Every 1–2 weeks in spring and summer; keep dry at other times

 Apply a cactus fertiliser every 4 weeks in spring and summer

 Periodically, tease out the hairs with a small, stiff brush to remove dust and other detritus

 In summer, but during dry weather only

Up to 4 weeks in spring and summer, longer at other times

COMPOST

 Standard cactus compost with added grit

// trim with sand, pebbles, grit or small stones to keep the base of the plant dry

WE JUST SIT THERE…

BROMELIAD

PUYA HUMILIS //

This prickly chap doesn't need much attention and will be happy on its own, even if you have to leave it for several weeks. It likes looking out of the window but isn't keen on damp, so prefers the living room or bedroom to the kitchen or bathroom. Best not get too close — the spines are sharp.

What is it?

bromeliad // A rosette-forming bromeliad from Bolivia where it grows on rocky slopes in the Andes

Take care of me...

Full light

Every 2–3 weeks in spring and summer; sparingly at other times

Apply a balanced fertiliser every 6–8 weeks in spring and summer

None required

Yes, during dry weather (can tolerate light frost if dry)

Up to 4 weeks in spring and summer; longer at other times

COMPOST

Standard bromeliad compost

// trim optional

WE JUST SIT THERE...

TILLANDSIA STRICTA // AIR PLANT

This diminutive creature is totally harmless and makes very few demands, apart from its periodic liking for a bath. Best to confine it, though, as it won't sit up straight in a pot so it can easily get knocked off a table and disappear up the vacuum cleaner.

What is it?

 air plant (bromeliad) // An epiphytic perennial with grey-green leaves from scrub and woodland in Venezuela and Trinidad to northern Argentina

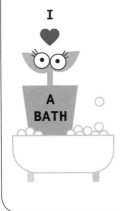

Take care of me...

 Full light but screened from strong sunlight through a window

 None required, but immerse the whole plant in tepid water for 1–2 hours every 3–4 weeks to refresh

 Mist with a liquid fertiliser at quarter strength every 4 weeks in spring and summer

 Remove any dead leaves

 No

 For up to 4 weeks in spring and summer; longer at other times

COMPOST

 Grow on a bed of dry pebbles or rocks in a bowl or jar

WE JUST SIT THERE…

Suitable
for: ♥   ♥ ♥

Very neglectful
types who like
to go out a lot

WE WOULD
CLIMB UP
THE WALL,
IF YOU
LET US

CLIMBER

JASMINUM POLYANTHUM // JASMINE

Given sufficient space, this climber could reach the ceiling but is easy to keep tame in a pot and can be trained and cut back to keep it within limits.

What is it?

climber // A climber from western China; twining stems are wreathed in scented white flowers from late winter to spring

Take care of me...

 Bright light but screened from direct sunlight through a window

 Every 1–2 weeks in spring and summer; water to keep the compost just moist at other times

 Apply a balanced fertiliser every 4 weeks in spring and summer

 Remove faded flowers; shorten overlong stems in summer

 Yes, during mild periods in summer

 Up to 2–3 weeks in spring and summer; up to 4 weeks at other times

COMPOST

Standard household compost

// trim optional

WE WOULD CLIMB UP THE WALL, IF YOU LET US

CLIMBER

STEPHANOTIS FLORIBUNDA // FLORADORA

Exuding class with its patent leather leaves, this seductive creature
will reel you in with the heady scent of its waxy, trumpet flowers.
No one can resist it.

What is it?

climber // A twining
climber from
tropical woodland
in Madagascar, with
white flowers from
spring to autumn

I ♥ LEAF SHINE

Take care of me...

 Bright light but screened
from direct sunlight through
a window

 Every 1—2 weeks in spring
and summer; mist daily, if
possible; keep just moist at
other times

 Apply a balanced fertiliser
every 2—3 weeks in spring
and summer

 Apply leaf shine, remove
any faded flowers; shorten
overlong stems in summer

 No

 Up to 2 weeks in spring
and summer; longer at
other times

COMPOST

Standard household compost

// a trim of moss will help keep the roots moist

WE WOULD CLIMB UP THE WALL, IF YOU LET US

CLIMBER

PHILODENDRON HEDERACEUM // HEARTLEAF PHILODENDRON

Upwardly mobile, this vigorous creature appreciates a tall scratching post to wrap its paws around as it clambers ever upwards. Inclined to be greedy, it can eat you out of house and home, if you're not careful.

What is it?

climber // A climbing perennial with large, heart-shaped leaves from the rainforest in Central America and the West Indies

I ♥ A GOOD

SCRATCH

Take care of me...

 Indirect light

 Liberally, every week in spring and summer; mist twice daily in summer; water more sparingly in winter

 Apply a balanced fertiliser every 4 weeks in spring and summer

 Apply leaf shine; shorten any overlong stems in summer

 No

 Up to 2 weeks in spring and summer; longer at other times

COMPOST

Standard household compost

// trim with moss to keep the roots moist

WE WOULD CLIMB UP THE WALL, IF YOU LET US

INDEX

ACKNOWLEDGEMENTS

Huge thanks to Christine Dugrenier and Adrian Baynes, who allowed photography in their beautiful apartment and cheerfully put up with the disruption that caused. Many thanks to Karolyn Andrews of Transform Communications, who arranged for Elho to supply several of the containers and other props used. Thanks also to editor Kathy Steer and designer Alice Chadwick who put the book together and saw it through to completion. Both were a pleasure to work with. I am also grateful to publisher Catie Ziller, who commissioned the project.

First published in 2019 by Hachette Livre, Marabout division
58, rue Jean-Bleuzen, 92178 Vanves Cedex, France

This edition published in 2021 by Smith Street Books
Naarm | Melbourne | Australia | smithstreetbooks.com

ISBN: 978-1-92241-7-060

For Smith Street Books
Publisher: Paul McNally
Proofreader: Ariane Durkin
Cover design: George Saad

Printed & bound in China by C&C Offset Printing Co., Ltd.

Book 160
10 9 8 7 6 5 4 3 2 1